PLAY IT
AS IT LIES

Allison & Busby Limited
12 Fitzroy Mews
London W1T 6DW
www.allisonandbusby.com

First published in 1987.
This edition published in Great Britain by Allison & Busby in 2014.

A CIP catalogue record for this book is available from
the British Library.

10 9 8 7 6 5 4 3 2 1

ISBN 978-0-7490-1711-8

Typeset in 10/15 pt Adobe Caslon Pro by
Allison & Busby Ltd.

The paper used for this Allison & Busby publication
has been produced from trees that have been legally sourced
from well-managed and credibly certified forests.

Printed and bound by
CPI Group (UK) Ltd, Croydon, CR0 4YY

CONTENTS

THE TRUTH
ABOUT GOLF

Golf is without doubt the easiest ball game
known to man.

If you can swat a fly with a rolled-up newspaper . . .

or knock the head off a daisy with a stick – you can
play golf.

The game requires no great physical strength . . .

or athletic ability.

It can be taken up at any age . . .

and provide a lifetime of enjoyment for all.

Some people take up golf in order to make
business contacts

. . . others to enjoy the fresh air and exercise.

Some see it as a means of escape
from domestic responsibilities.

To others it is an aid to social climbing.

Whatever his motivation, however, one thing
is certain – the golfer is a happy man

. . . provided, of course, that he does not start reading about how to do it

or seeking the advice of experts.

TALKING GOLF

It is important that the aspiring golfer learns
the meaning of certain golfing terms, so that he can
understand what his fellow sportsmen are saying to him.

This man is 'hitting three off the tee'.

This one is 'blasting out of a bunker'.

This is known as 'a dog leg' (or casual water).

It is best dealt with by the 'pitch and run shot'.

Here is 'a downhill lie'

and a 'golfing widow'.

This is 'a full member'.

This player is 'taking a free drop'.

They are both now 'pin high'

and taking 'the nap of the green'.

This sportsmen is 'playing through the green'.

This one is 'playing around'.

'Bounce' is an integral part of the game

. . . so is 'the rub of the green'.

Hitting the ball as far as you can up the fairway
is known as 'the long game'.

Putting out on the green is called 'the short game'.

'Direction post.'

RULES AND
ETIQUETTE

It is essential that you address your ball with care before driving off – so that you can recognise it at all times.

Failure to identify your own ball may lead
to frayed tempers

or flouting of the rules of golf.

It is unforgivable to use gamesmanship on the
golf course – either by ill-timed noises . . .

. . . or questionable actions.

Dress and equipment should be neat and practical

. . . eccentric clothing may tend to interfere with play.

Do not attempt to replace your divots on the teeing ground otherwise the green sward may become loose and powdery.

Once on the fairway, however, all divots must be firmly
replaced to discourage scavenging birds.

You are not permitted to accept physical assistance
when playing your shots

. . . or to be sheltered from the elements when doing so.

You may not move earth or rocks to improve
your stance . . .

and wilful destruction of growing vegetation
is against the rules.

Golf is a game of trust and you will often find yourself
alone with your conscience.

Remember that if you move your ball by accident
you are deemed to have played another shot.

You are required to fill in any hollows
you have made in bunkers.

Hand warmers are legal but must not be used
to warm anything else.

You may not use mechanical gadgets to assess
wind speed and direction

. . . but you are permitted to toss a little grass
into the air.

It is your right to declare your ball unplayable at any time – provided that your declaration can be heard by everyone concerned.

GOLF IN
THE GARDEN

'It went straight down the waste disposal unit.'

GOLF IN
THE HOME

'That's where the pain gets me, doc.'

GOLF IN
THE OFFICE

'Sometimes I think you love your golf more
than you love me, Mr Pilkington.'

'How do you like being on the board of directors, Wilkins?'

'Don't you *ever* relax, J. B. ?'

'Who's responsible for this shoddy thing?'

'What the hell's going on on the shop floor?'

'I said, can I have my ball back, please?'

'When did you start feeling that people
were ignoring you?'

LADIES' GAME

'Would you help me with my zipper please?'

'I've got a hole in one.'

'Hand me a number eight iron.'

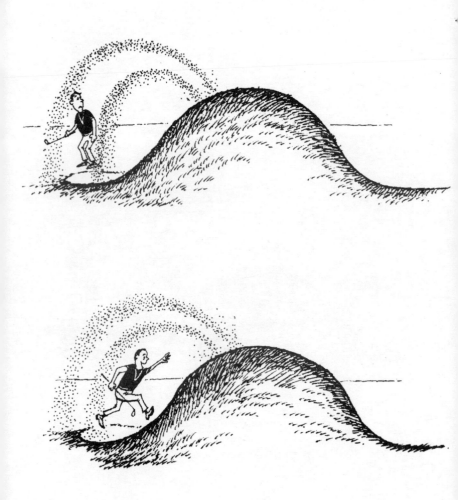

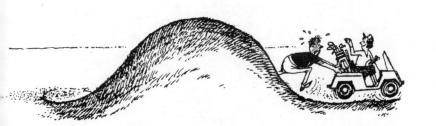

'FORE!'

'I notice it's always *my* ball you accidentally drive over.'

'We found her ball but now she's lost an earring.'

'We found her earring then bang went her beads.'

A NATURAL HISTORY FOR GOLFERS

Most golfers spend many hours communing with nature. Here is a simple guide to make it even more enjoyable.

FLORA

SEMI-ROUGH. All grasses, weeds and wild flowers from about four to eight inches in height belong to the genus semi-rough. Any players slicing into it can usually be seen giving thanks for a narrow escape.

DEEP ROUGH. A very varied family of plants up to five and more feet in height. Golfers can frequently be heard calling them by a wide variety of incorrect names.

Nº 4 WOOD

Nº 3 WOOD

Nº 1 WOOD

Nº 2 WOOD

WOODS. Nos. 1, 2, 3 and 4 woods are the names given to collections of trees which have a strange attraction for golf balls. Most golfers find that three woods are quite enough.

DECIDUOUS WOODS. Drop all their leaves in the autumn
so that any ball that comes to rest in them is lost for
six months at least.

CONIFEROUS WOODS. Keep their leaves firmly in place and make it so dark that it is impossible to find a ball at any time of the year.

FAUNA

RABBITS. The cuddly little creatures can be seen digging holes all over the countryside.

TIGERS. Almost never seen in the woods but can
frequently be spotted moving very fast down the fairway.

FERRETS. A common sight on the golf course – chipping off the fairway onto the putting green.

GAME. Usually erupts suddenly from the woods.

PAR. A young salmon which you may be lucky enough to spot if you have sliced into a river.

BIRDIE. A tiny creature that sings its heart out to charm the nature lover.

EAGLE. Rarely seen except on Scottish courses.

ALBATROSS. If you ever hit one of these you will remember it for the rest of your life.

WOODPECKER. Can be seen and heard on most courses
rapping away on the trees.

USEFUL TIPS

When big money is at stake, top golfers find it well
worthwhile to employ professional caddies.

A visor is very helpful when trying to follow the flight of your ball.

It is courteous to watch the flight of your opponent's
ball also – so that you can tell him where it landed.

Never park your golf trolley in inconvenient places

... or drive your golf buggy without due care
and attention.

Remember that you are allowed to abandon a game if
there is a danger of being struck by lightning

. . . or if a player becomes seriously indisposed.

Do not get depressed if you are not playing
your best game

and *never* take your spite out on other people.
After all . . .

golf is only a game.

ALSO IN THE SERIES

The perfect gift for any angler who appreciates the primitive thrill of hunting wild creatures, the hours spent studying minute aquatic flies, and the art of manipulating his tackle. Britain's beloved cartoonist Norman Thelwell creates reels of fun in his rip-roaring angler's guide.

The perfect gift for any gardener who has experienced overbearing neighbours, the pains of building a water feature, unruly indoor plants; and the battle to dig the lawnmower out from the shed. Britain's beloved cartoonist Norman Thelwell presents a fine crop of witticisms in his hilarious gardener's handbook.

The perfect gift for any sailor who has misinterpreted a distress signal, worn stilettos on board, abandoned ship, or experienced irreparable damage to their social status at the club. Britain's beloved cartoonist Norman Thelwell will have you in fits of luffter with his indispensable manual of instruction for sailors everywhere.

To discover more great books and to
place an order visit our website at
www.allisonandbusby.com

Don't forget to sign up to our free newsletter at
www.allisonandbusby.com/newsletter
for latest releases, events and exclusive offers

Allison & Busby Books
@AllisonandBusby

You can also call us on
020 7580 1080
for orders, queries
and reading recommendations